BUT His Love!

Pookie

authorHOUSE®

AuthorHouse™
1663 Liberty Drive
Bloomington, IN 47403
www.authorhouse.com
Phone: 1 (800) 839-8640

Published by AuthorHouse 12/04/2017

ISBN: 978-1-5462-1896-8 (sc)
ISBN: 978-1-5462-1895-1 (e)

Library of Congress Control Number: 2017918157

Print information available on the last page.

This book is printed on acid-free paper.

Dedication

This book is dedicated to all of you who think that you have to struggle with things even after you're saved but you don't. You will go through stuff, but God is always there for you. This story is the book of my life, my very first book, so excuse me if I chase rabbits. I want to thank the Publisher and the Editor who have put all these pieces of my book together and made it an awesome book. I pray that no weapon formed against myself or my colleagues shall prosper right now, or that anything will stop this book from being published this year in Jesus Name. I also want to dedicate this book to Pastors who came from New York and gave me an awesome Word. In my book, I will mention names, because I want to be comfortable when telling my story of what I know from the beginning to the end.

Acknowledgements

I would like to thank and acknowledge the best editor in the whole wide world, my Sister in Christ, who is beautiful and intelligent, and a mighty woman of God who took time out of her life to help me put mine on paper; Free Indeed Church, Apostle and Prophetess, who were there for me during my time of spiritual drought, and who implanted seeds of God's Word into my life; And to all of the Saints in my life for teaching me a deeper foundation of gifts and callings, and immersing me in her everlasting love. To my God-parents and my sister who took me in when no one else would, and taught me how to be a woman; my family members and friends who put up with my spiritual purging I was going through, and those who still love me no matter what; and to my best friend Tinkem, a love note thanking you for loving me while I was locked up in my dark places. You were the best listner that I had, and you implanted the Word of God in me while on the inside of that place of shame, and showed me how to truly follow Jesus by applying and acting on His Word. And even when you were released before I was, you continued to love me not only as a sister in Christ, but as a true sister and loving friend who always loved and understood me when no one else could.

Contents

Foreword

Pookie is an example of a woman who has not only been tried in the fire of life, but has shown proof that the fire won't keep her down. She is a woman of God whose past will make many cry, but her victories will instill so much hope for a better future. I have been so humbled after being asked to edit her book, going through each chapter of her life, and can't help but to believe that the way she is has to do with the Holy Spirit. He has given her beauty, knowledge, intelligence, and a sense of humor that will have your stomach hurting from so much laughter. pookie is the Author of this book, her testimony. I'm so thankful to have another sister in my life, and that I had the time to walk with her on this assignment.

Introduction

JESUS IS LORD. Jesus IS the Living Word.

Everything that comes from Him cannot be voided out because Jesus is the very Breath of God. He's the Logos. He's God's Son. He IS God; Father, Son and Holy Spirit. Throughout this book, I will be addressing the Father as, "Abba", "My Father", "Jesus". Sometimes, I will emphasize "Best Friend", "The Holy Spirit", My Counselor", and "Helper". To me, God forms Holy Spirit as a "her". For me He forms that part of Himself as a woman... you'll see why.

Chapter One

Pookie

"Before I formed you in the womb I knew you; Before you were born I sanctified you; I ordained you a prophet to the nations" (Jeremiah 1:5). "For You formed my inward parts; You covered me in my mother's womb" (Psalms 139:30, NKJV). I love the New King James Version because it isn't watered down, and there's nothing taken out.

In the year 1983, December the 2nd, I was born to a woman named Terry Thomas. She had me when she was incarcerated in Texas. I don't know why she was incarcerated, but I do know she was struggling with addiction; smoking crack. I was born in a Hospital, that was a low-income hospital. As a matter of fact, 1983 was the last year it was in existence. I was named after my Mom because she didn't have time to name me. Before she could name me, people were grabbing me out of her arms to take me to Child Protective Services, I believe she was calling to let people know she had me, because if they wouldn't have been able to contact anyone to come and get me, I definitely would have ended up in Child Protective Services. So, they contacted her brother, my Uncle Leo, who had been visiting her while she was in jail. My Uncle on my mom side knew where my Dad was, so he went to go tell him that I was born. At the time, my Dad was at the store because he and my mom weren't getting along. Mom was in her addiction with crack cocaine, and as a result, I was deemed a crack baby. So, my dad contacted my Aunt Carla and Big Mamma another word for Grandma. You will hear a lot about Big Momma in this book. She was my God-given Mom. So, Aunt Carla, Big Momma, and my Dad came to pick me up from the hospital. They took me home and cared for me. My time after being born was split between living with Big Momma and Aunt Carla, because Big Momma didn't have a house built yet. After some time, Big Momma was able to get the money to have her house built, something she always wanted to do. But there were some things going on with my Grandmother at the time of my birth which hindered Big Momma's dream house.

In the beginning, I was living with Aunt Carla. She had two girls, my cousins Lisa and Stacie, the oldest. Across the way in the same apartment complex were my Aunts Sandy and Francen. As a young child, I lived among three different places, which I thought was pretty bad even though I had a big family. There were four women raising me before the age of five. Shortly thereafter, I began living with Big Momma permanently until the age of eleven. I remember my childhood memories, going to school and wondering why my Mom and Dad weren't there to pick me up. Big Momma really couldn't afford me, but she loved me so she kept me. But she was breaking down, because you must understand that Big Momma got me while at the age of 65 to take care of me; had been diagnosed with cancer three different times and had been in a bad car accident. However, she was my Big Momma and took care of me in spite of all of that.

This chapter is mainly about Big Momma and I. Texas is where I grew up. Big Momma would always bathe me in the morning. We were poor, so when we moved in the new house that she had built, it wasn't finished. I mean, she literally didn't even have the walls covered. There was nothing but the roof over our heads, and you could see through the walls, but that was her house and she wanted to live in it. Big Momma would always have something for me to eat in the morning, noon, and evening time. I remember when Time Tree's used to sell their ice cream cones. She would always take me by there to get one after church. Big Momma was a woman of God. She stayed in the church, loved the Lord, and would always sing to God; and I know that was the first time I was introduced to God.

She would always pray. I remember when I was little I used to have these bad headaches and didn't know why. I would say to her, "Hey Big

Momma, I have a headache." And she would say, "Oh baby, come on over here and lay by me." So I would go to her and would lay my head on her chest. She was so soft and warm because of her age. And she would place her hands on my forehead and pray, "In the Name of Jesus", and all my headaches and troubles would go away. Big Momma was kind of like my Safe Haven as a little girl. I remember those times I used to "cut up", a Big Momma phrase that meant I was being bad, because I spoke out loud, sometimes with no one being there. But, I always thought in my mind, "Who was I talking to?" I was talking to somebody, not sure if I was talking to my guardian angel but I wasn't talking to myself. *I was* talking to somebody.

If there was anything I wanted, Big Momma would try her best to get it for me. But if she couldn't, I would be satisfied with what she did. As I mentioned before, being very poor, I didn't have normal Christmases like everyone else. My cousins, you know, had good Christmases; they got the presents. All I had some Christmases was when Big Momma would take me down to the Helps Center. She was older and would take me on that bus and we would ride it there. We would stand in line and I was so happy to get a present. Sometimes we would stand in line, and many of those years I wasn't able to get one. But some way, somehow, God kept us. Although at the time, I didn't know it was God because I was too little.

I was a problem-child in school because I always got in trouble. And I used to get picked on when I was little. At the age of eight, I was very mischievous. One day, I almost burned down the house trying to light the candles on my birthday cake. Big Momma told me not to mess with the cake, but I messed with it anyway, very rebellious. It was a Little Mermaid cake, my very first birthday cake and I loved it! And I lit that cake up because I wanted it that badly. Although I didn't know God, Big Momma said I used to play alone and act like I was preaching. I remember back then, going around preaching the Word of God, then passing the pretend offering plate when finished.

There are specific things I do remember that stick out from my past, like playing "Momma and Daddy" with my cousins. Who didn't play "Momma and Daddy" with their cousins? Child experimentation. There was a time when I was four years old and my Dad picked me up to spend the night, and I was molested by this woman. My innocence was stripped from me, just stripped! Now when I look back, I know God had a great destiny for me. Oh how the enemy would send a slimy, nasty, perverted, demon to have sex with me, and destroy my innocence! I never told anyone because I was told not to tell. While still young, my Dad used to have sex with women when I was around. I would be under the covers acting like I was asleep, but could see and hear everything. Man, I was introduced to all kinds of sex demons when I was little.

Fastforwarding to when I was ten years old, Big Momma was involved in a car accident that crippled her. It was reported that she flew out of the car, and that's why she couldn't walk. I think that's when I started losing my best friend. Its seemed like after the accident, everything started going bad for her, but she held on. I have a memory of her when she was standing with her cane by the refrigerator. This was one of those days she sent me to Cullen to get groceries at the age of nine, that was a very long walk for me. When I would return, I would do things around the house for her. She continued to love me through all she was dealing with. One time, she fell. Then her falls became frequent. She would always fall! And I was so helpless because I couldn't help her. Although I was little, I would try to help her up, but she would yell at me, "Get back!" "Go!" "Go back over there Pookie, go back over there!" And I would look at her, hoping she would get up. After the result of her falls, Big Momma could no longer take care of me. Then I had to go live with Aunt Laurie. There are two more memories to share about Big Momma, before I move on to my new guardian. When I used to play in the grass, she would let out a sound, "WOOO-WOOOOOO," that was her signal to let me know she wanted something, or for me to come in the house. But while I sat in the grass, I would look at the clouds, and I know my guardian angel was out there with me. Even in the midst of all that, that had went on with my Dad and Big Momma, God still protected me. He foreknew me. He predestined me in my mother's womb to be there for me; to be His child, to spread His Gospel. There was another time when I was on the swing by a tree that had a bunch of snakes around it. The angels would protect me while I was by myself on the swing that was on the other side of the house; the same angel who looked at the clouds with me; the same angel who would push me on the swing is still watching me, protecting me.

As I got older, I didn't like reading the Bible. I really didn't like reading period, because I didn't know how to read. So I grew up in school not knowing how to read or write. But Big Momma taught me Math and how to write my name. I entered into the adolescent stage, still rebellious, and began to start worrying about why I didn't have a Mom; why I wasn't like everybody else; why wasn't I rich like they were; why wasn't I pretty. But that's for the next chapter. So Big Momma bought me this rabbit and I scared the rabbit was so bad because I kept picking it up that it die on me. This is the first time I grabbed the Bible and tried to revive the rabbit. It was Easter. Now I know that bunnies don't have anything to do with the Blood and Resurrection of Jesus, Thank You Jesus!! One day, Big Momma said, "Go take that rabbit outside! That rabbit dead!" That hurt me so bad. She must have told me over and over again to "Leave the rabbit alone!" "You're making it nervous!", "You're making it poo-poo!" "Leave that rabbit alone!" I just wanted to touch the rabbit. I was alone and didn't have any friends to play with. But on that day, the rabbit died on me, eyes wide open and bucked. He got scared and had a heart attack.

I was growing up and Big Momma was still getting older, and unable to take care of me anymore. That's why Aunt Laurie started coming around more. She would pick me up and take me to the country and I would spend nights with her. Those were the times when we were good.

Chapter Two

Lying, Stealing, and Suicide - Part 1

"This evil people, who refuse to hear My words, who follow the dictates of their hearts, and walk after other gods to serve them and worship them, shall be just like this ash which is profitable for nothing." (Jeremiah 13:10)

In this second chapter, I'm going to be talking about a time in my life when I was doing a lot of lying, stealing, and even tried to commit suicide. It all started when I began living with my Aunt Laurie. Aunt Laurie is the oldest on my Dad's side. She took me in when Big Momma became too sick to care for me. I was really excited to go live in the country with her. She would come and pick me up and take me there to visit all the time when I lived with Big Momma. As I think back, I remember being very rebellious during the ages of eleven and twelve. While living with my Aunt, I attended middle school, junior high, and high school. And during that time, I attended, but that will be addressed in part two of this chapter. I didn't know while my aunt cared for me that she was receiving money to keep me. But, of course it would make sense because she had an extra mouth to feed, so she would need checks anyway for my care. It was an adjustment for me to settle in because I was missing Big Momma, but I was happy at the same time because I was going to a new school. This school was a culture shock for me because the majority of the population was Caucasian, and I wasn't familiar with that particular environment being a young girl from a predominantly Black school. I went to Grommer Elementary school in the fourth grade, after finishing third grade at Grant Elementary, a school that no longer stands. Then the rebellion began; getting into trouble at school and not being able to go to recess. I also had problems with being accepted by people. Growing up, I had a fear of reading; and the enemy used that as a weapon against me during that time, telling me, "You're nothing. You don't know how to read." I remember one time when my stealing habit began, Aunt Laurie was working at the prison as a prison guard with her friend named Ms. Thomas. Now, these two ladies resided in the same town, worked together, and had decided to partner up and open a daycare. All went according to plan in the process, but when it came time for the daycare to open, things began to fall apart. I remember my Aunt telling me as a little girl, "Hey, if you work at the daycare, I'm gonna pay you to work there." I began to work there like she suggested. But after I had worked there for some time, I realized I wasn't getting paid. So, you know what I did? I started stealing. I stole money from her purse, and spent it, then started giving money to the kids at school who I wanted to be friends with; stuff like that. Trouble at school progressed; cursing out the teacher and not wanting to do anything I was told. And at the same time, I was lost, still wanting my Mommy and Daddy. There was one incident when I had called another little girl the "b" word. But I lied and said I called her a "fitch." I said, "I called her fitch, I didn't call her that". Nevertheless, I got in trouble for it. As a result, all my Christmas presents that year were taken away when that happened, because that was the last straw. I was so mad at Aunt Laurie, I thought she hated me. To me, that was such a drastic punishment. She took all of my presents to the daycare and said she was going to give them away there, but not before letting me see them all in the bag that she took them in. To make matters worse, I'm working at the daycare and I see all the toys that were mine being given away. All the while, I traveled back and forth from my Aunt's house to visit Big Momma. During one visit there, I caught the Chicken Pox and they made me stay there until all the bumps were gone. I loved visiting Big Momma, spending nights there and spending time with my family. One summer, I visited her and my Uncle Edward, one of my Dad's brothers, while he was living in the area where Big Momma was. I was outside playing, and I had climbed a tree, fell down, and broke both of my wrists. Because I needed screws in both my wrists, Aunt Laurie told me that I couldn't go back to visit my Big Mama, because I didn't know how to stay out of trouble and out of the trees.

Even at a young age, I thought about killing myself. I felt like nobody loved me because I was bad. My mind was warped; the enemy had so much control over my mind as he fed me so many lies about how I wasn't worth anything... "You can't read," "You don't have a family," "You're living with an Aunt who doesn't love you." I started taking prescription pills, not knowing what the prescription was for; attempted seven or six times. One time I focused that hurt on one of my cousins and tried to poison her. This behavior took its toll on me for the worst. I would be at home and not clean up or do anything, just there. I felt worthless. Like, why was I here? I knew I was rebellious, and I was stuck at the house not being able to go anywhere; places like the fair and other places that normal kids were able to go to. My Aunt always kept me in the house and I felt that wasn't fair as a teenager. I should have been able to get out and go places. I ran away from home twice, telling her, "I hate you!" "I don't love you, I hate you!" That's when our relationship became broken, especially on her end because she took what I said personally and not the way a grown up should have. I felt that she made sure that my life was miserable. She would always talk about me to my other Aunts.

I always received hand-me-downs even though my Aunt Laurie cared for me. She was receiving checks for me, but I hardly ever saw anything that was bought with the money. She rarely bought me new clothes because she spent that money on herself. My respect for her was gone. I used to sneak boys in the house and have sex with them, smoke weed in the house, and lie to her about all of it.

She and I always fought and she would try to whip me. My mind wasn't right back then. I stole something every day. When Aunt Laurie was in charge at the rodeo, I would steal stuff out of her purse. I took her jewelry to school to try and buy friendship from students who weren't my friends. Another thing the enemy held over my head was the fact that I attended Resource Class, because I wasn't smart enough to keep up in the regular classes. This made me feel dumb; incompetent; fearful of people despite the fact that I was home-schooled by Big Momma in my early years and was doing fine in school while with her. But transferring to high school while living with Aunt Laurie was not as successful after taking in the lies of the enemy about not being able to do anything and being a nobody.

As my overall rebellion spiraled downward, I went to live with my Aunt Carla in the south of Texas and attended my sophomore year of high school there. However, my rebellious behavior with boys started at this new school and my promiscuity hastened. During that time I lost weight and I was feeling myself, couldn't nobody tell me anything! And I lost my virginity on my birthday to somebody I didn't even like! This particular day, I was hanging out with this girl, and we were at her house, not knowing that this particular boy was going to come over. At the time, I didn't know that she was giving up her body while I hung out over there. I just thought she was cool. So this boy and I had sex because I wanted to lose my virginity on my birthday. That's how bad my mind was. To add to my mess, I was stealing from my cousins while living with Aunt Carla. I rebelled so much and did so many things that people couldn't forgive me for it. But I know God forgave me, and I apologized to everyone involved. This can't be held against me anymore. Once you apologize and receive Jesus Christ as your Savior, and people don't want to forgive you, then so be it. There's nothing you can do. You just keep moving forward and keep praying for them. Ask God to change their heart. That's it. Well, my time spent with Aunt Charlotta was up, and I moved back to with Aunt Laurie to try again. I started going back to church, St. Paul, joined the drill team at school, and connected with my Godparents, Mr. & Mrs. Smith.

Chapter Three

Lying, Stealing, and Suicide - Part 2

The Smith's took me in and I began living with them. I was still going to Church, but was only playing Church. Saints, I wasn't saved at that time. So the lying, stealing, and contemplating suicide continued. Although I never stole from the Smith's, I lied to them and stole from other people by trying to be slick with credit cards. During my stay there, I went to prom, graduated from high school, and signed up for Healer College in, Texas. And all during this time, my destructive behavior never stopped. This is how the enemy continued to warp my mind. When I got to college, I started making friends, but my lying behavior never stopped. I was trying to be someone that I wasn't.

My education suffered because all I was there for was the drinking, guys, parties, and sex. However, I did meet a guy named Derrick Fild Jr, the first guy I ever fell in love with. He was from Georgia, but was born in Illinois. After we met, we started having sex all the time. That was just something to do. I would wear trampy clothes while entertaining him and his friends, being flirtatious with no respect for myself. Derrick and his friends would go a lot of places and rob them for money. I was robbing too, but you will read about that later. I thought that Derrick was a really cool guy, but all and all, he was a troublemaker, and I didn't want to see him in that light. I saw him as someone who could love me because I loved him. We fell in lust because of the drinking and going different places with each other. I could have gotten killed going to some of those places with some of those people from college, but God kept me. Because my academics had greatly suffered due to my irresponsibility, Wiley expelled me from college. Derrick was expelled also. After that, I moved back in with Aunt Laurie and started back working at her day care, not really doing much with my life. I needed a place to stay after getting kicked out of college, and she was the only person I had that I could go to. It didn't take long for me to start growing tired of living there with her.

Chapter Four

Family Drama and Church

I grew up as a young girl without a Father and Mother, not saying I didn't have them but they were absent; hearing that my Mom was a crackhead living under a bridge and later finding out about other kids; and being raised by my Great Grandmother, the Love of my life who took me in; mother, companion, friend; she was given to me by God, without a doubt.

Family Drama. This where the spirit of rejection began to take hold of my life. He already planted a seed at birth because I was abandoned by my Mother and Father; and the seed grew as I did. My Aunt Laruie was a very mean lady, and I believe that's where the meanness within me came from. She would always yell at people saying stuff like, "Get back from the tv!" And, "Don't fix your face like that, you're gonna be ugly!" She was always like that towards me. The only thing good she did was teach me my ABC's, that's about it. Also, growing up with cousins who had both their parents present had an effect on me. I found out around the age of fifteen during an argument with one of my cousins that my Father was gay. Later in life, I found out that my Mom was a lesbian. Fussing and fighting was a steady part of life as I got older. One time around the age of twenty-one, drunk and high, I was invited with my ex-fiance Kaleb to my Aunt's house. After we got there, my Aunt caught him rolling up weed on her patio. She became mad, and had every right to be, because she had other company over her house from work. I got mad and wanted to fight her, told her that she wasn't nothing; and went over to her daughter, my cousin, and told her that I would kill her if I ever talked to her again. There were so many mean things that came out of my mouth because I was under the influence, but also lost and empty; a very evil person with a lot of witchcraft in me. I was practicing a little bit during my early twenties.

Going back to when I was a little girl, I was molested three times by three different people. The first time was by my Dad's girlfriend when I was four years old. That made me feel like I did something wrong and I was in it with her, so I didn't tell. The second time was sexually assaulted by my Uncle when I lived with my Aunt Laurie. He lied to the police and said that he didn't touch me. There were others during instances where I was almost raped but I was able to protect myself and escape. Being sexual was a part of me since I was little. My Dad used to have sex with other girls in front of me, so the sexual immorality spirits of Incubus and Succubus were attached to me early on. I was deprived of my innocence being in that type of environment; thinking about sex all the time, condoms lying all on the floor for all to see. Finally, there was a time when I did get to stay with my Dad around the age of six. I was sexually active at that time, wanting to play "Mommy and Daddy" all the time with my cousins. We would wait until our Aunties left to pull out hidden tapes with masterbation and sex scenes, exploring and doing things we had no business doing. The enemy had planted those seeds in our heads at a young age. There was a time when I tried to take advantage of someone younger than I was as a child; a ripple effect of demonic spirits. I just thank God that I'm not in that frame of mind anymore. He took that from me. A lot of things that kids are exposed to can turn them into monsters that are not of God. The enemy starts when you're young. He likes to get a hold of you when you're innocent. But it's only the Cross of Jesus that can break that thing. I was wondering why it took a while for me to record this part of the book, but it had been because of the hurt.

That hurt manifest into the thoughts of suicide. The spirit of rejection started to take its toll on me, especially being around everyone during who had their Mothers there helping them. I didn't have that Mother, or that Father. It was almost like I was ungrateful for the Big

Momma that I did have. Everybody knew I was her favorite, but I didn't appreciate her in the way that I should have because of the hurt as a little girl. And that hurt followed me into my adulthood because of the rejection. As mentioned earlier, I lost my virginity on my birthday. The spirit of rejection was every place of my life where I was rejected, and I found acceptance in sex. If it was with a man it was filling the void of Fatherhood, or if it was with a woman it filled the void of Motherhood. I was missing the love of a Father and Mother that I never received as a child. So, the way I would numb that pain was by sexual experiences, and I would have sex with people I barely knew.

Going back to losing my virginity on my birthday; I didn't actually lose it with the first guy. There was another guy after him named Travis and I lost it with him. My.. how the enemy had me bound! It was so crazy because when I had sex with Travis, I wanted to lose my virginity so that I could have sex and not be a virgin with another guy who like me! That was so demonic! Just a demonic scheme, a plan with all these soul ties attached to me through these events in my life. And it was downhill from there. I was ready to have fun and have sex over and over again; and thought I was safe because I didn't have a whole lot of sex in a year, according to my understanding. My warped cycle was to meet guys, have sex with them, and call that love. Then I began to hook up with the wrong people; guys picked me up to go have sex in the motel and bought me things as a reward. When I returned to my Aunt Laurie's, I had sex with one of my boyfriends outside of Church on New Year's Day. While out there on the grass, my cousin caught us.

I would use a guy as my hero because I thought that after all the times I had given my body to guys that at some point I would land one of them to have for myself. That's how corrupt the enemy had my mind, telling me, "You're gonna land you one, a knight in shining armor baby." And I sure did land me one, Kaleb. He was from another world, up North in Philadelphia, and he had me wrapped around his finger just like the enemy wanted him to have me wrapped. So wrapped, in fact, that he would use me, head butt me, and then have sex with me. This man had me robbing places with him, one place was Soup's Donuts. Now, you know something isn't right when you resort to robbing a donuts place! I was so lost, but I knew I loved him because I felt like he protected me and he loved me. He gave me the attention that I needed. And all that time while I was with him, I was disrespectful to my Big Momma; yelling at her, not going home on time. She locked me out and called the police on me because I was stealing, sneaking boys in the house and having sex while she was in the other room. I was so disrespectful. Sex was always on my mind, all while looking for Prince Charming; doing things I knew I had no business doing because I'm trying to fill the void of rejection with sex. People weren't really fond of me because I was a troublemaker. I turned my cousin against me because I told her I was gonna kill her mom, and that's something she's still dealing with today. As a result, I asked her and God for forgiveness, but so far only God has forgiven me. That's something she will have to work on with God.

On the Church end of things, I wasn't attending during this time but I knew right from wrong. While robbing these different places with Kaleb, I became addicted to cocaine. I loved to snort powder, and I was also addicted to weed. People say that you can't get addicted to weed, but yes you can. Alcohol was ever present as well. I couldn't get myself to try crack because of my Mom, but little did I know I was headed that direction. My choice of pills were Xanax and Ecstasy. One night I was at my apartment I was about to lose, because I didn't want to go out and find a job. I was on the floor and was about to overdose due to snorting over an eightball of cocaine and having sex with Kaleb, feeling nothing. I wanted him to get off me because I felt like I was about to die. So he got up and I went into the livingroom. My heart was beating so fast and I could hardly breathe. I dropped to the floor pleading to God saying, "God, please! Jesus, please! I don't want to be like my Mom living under a bridge! I don't want to be strung out on drugs! I want to be somebody!" And I asked him to save me, to help me. I told Him that I didn't want to die like that.

Chapter Five

Wicked Mind

This chapter will expose the wicked mind frame that the enemy will have you operating in. I didn't know at the time I was working in that; however, this is also a part of my testimony.

I was my worst enemy when it came to my thoughts about me, I brought myself down. And because I used to think of so many bad things about myself, I just knew that other people talked about me. However, my mindset was that way because there were people who really did talk about me. This was one of the tactics the enemy used against me because I believed what they said, even though they didn't know me. I would hear awful things as I grew up like, "You get on my nerves," "You're ugly," and I knew I wasn't ugly... "You ain't got your Momma or your Daddy," You're poor," "You stink," "Y'all don't have no toothbrush or toothpaste to brush your yellow teeth," "Y'all live in a raggedy house in the ghetto," "You had to go to the Helps Center to get stuff," just nagging. The spirit of python was manifested through all these people who were always talking down on me. As I got older, the things I heard were "You're a hoe," "You're a prostitute," "You're dumb," "You're in Resource classes," "You can't read"...so many ugly things were said throughout my childhood that entered into my adolescent and womanhood stages in life. Those things came from the some of my family who were supposed to love me.

I was very misunderstood because of the way my mind was set. It was warped by the enemy because of my upbringing, believing all the lies that were spoken through other vessels who were around me that I didn't deserve Goodness. I grew up thinking that I didn't deserve anything good like everybody else, because I didn't have it good. The foundation of my wicked mind was believing that my circumstances determined who I was and it defined me. But that was a lie from the enemy. It did not define me. I began to think that I was worthless and I tried suicide, because of my thinking that no one would love me unless I gave up my body for sex. For eight years, I was a bisexual who had affairs with married women and men; and was engaged at one time and slept around during that relationship. I had no morals or respect for myself back then. So wicked, I didn't care. People used to call me "Heartbreaker Pookie" because I was so bad, no caring about anybody's feelings. My attitude toward my victims was that they would get over it…"Oh well," was my mindset. I could hold a grudge against anyone and it was so bad. Looking back, it was due to bitterness, envy, and jealousy of other people around me; unforgiveness and unrepentance made me feel like I was suffocating and I couldn't breathe. I was my worst enemy because of my wicked mind! I would try to read and I couldn't pronounce a word, yet listening to the enemy telling me mess like, "You'll never know how to read," "You're too old not to know how to read," "Uh oh, the teacher is gonna call on you to read, you're gonna get stuck and embarrassed." Instead of encouraging myself to learn different words each day that will help me learn how to read, I believed the lies of Satan.

I was a class clown in high school because I felt like nobody liked me. So, I had to make fun of other people in order for someone to like me. Wicked thinking. Any type of thinking that makes you want to harm yourself, that's nothing but the enemy. The devil had me wanting to commit suicide, do you hear me? Because nobody gave me attention. This is about wicked thinking. There was a time when I wanted to be by myself, not knowing at the time why I felt that way, but found out later it was because I was being entertained…entertained by demons that wanted to take me out; making me feel like a was a nobody. No matter what I looked like on the outside, pretty, skinny, it didn't matter. I felt like I was a nobody. I didn't know how to read, and I didn't even know how to clean myself appropriately in my twenties; so ignorant about many things, and was easily influenced by negative crowds. The girls would tell me to come with them and get high, and I was right there with them. They would tell me to go drive down to different places with them to go score some cocaine, and I would jump at the chance.

I moved to California,which is 3days away from Texas. that when a really started running away. I was running away from Healer College, where my drinking, drugs and sex escapades were rampant with Derrick. We went so many places together not thinking about what might happen. I could have gotten killed in Georgia because so many girls up there liked him. They could have beaten me up, kidnapped me, anything. Wicked thinking. One time I took a solo trip back to Georgia, and was staying with somebody else in the BTW apartments who I didn't even know. I didn't know anyone in Georgia. That's how bad Satan had my mind, just had me running from state to state and I didn't even know what I was running from. While there, I started a relationship with this guy from New York. He sold drugs and had brought some to me in his backpack and told me to start selling it. I told him that I can't be selling drugs for him. It was something in me that held me back from doing that, besides, he wanted me to sell them from where I was staying. Wicked thinking. I was talking to three guys at the same time; Derrick, the guy with the apartment, and the New Yorker, and could have gotten myself killed out there because I didn't really know that Georgia mindset. One guy looked at me showing attention, and I started talking to him...a little hoodrat in the ghetto going from house to house meeting different people, being so friendly. But I see now how God protected me and how that friendliness allowed me to hang out with anybody there. People felt comfortable to be around me and weren't fearful. Even the ones who looked at me crazy when I first got there started to come around. I had nothing to offer them because I was homeless in Georgia. Everywhere I went I was homeless. I didn't want to do anything but wanted everybody to take care of me. Nobody took care of me in college so I flew to Georgia to find someone who could. Just crazy! But God kept me while on those Travelhound buses. He kept me in those dark alleys. He saved me from myself, robbing all those places. Wicked mind. The Lord's Word says that He saves us from our destruction. Wow! The mindframe I was in; sleeping with men and women, popping pills and snorting powder...JESUS! I was destined to die! I'm sharing this chapter because I know there are others out there, and I know the tricks of the enemy and how he has people's minds like mine was.

I didn't trust anybody because I didn't trust me. And I didn't know what love was because I was too consumed with my hurt from the past to allow anyone to love or talk to me. I held things in after being abused. So when I got older, I started talking any kind of way I wanted to, and nobody was going to talk to me any kind of way unless they were ready for a fight. I wasn't taught how to express myself around people who loved me. I just held it in, feeling I was guilty of something when I wasn't. For some reason, it seemed like every October I would get in trouble for something. The enemy had a plan and I could feel the plan he had set, because I felt I had already did something anyway. I came to the conclusion that my reaping season was in October. Last year in 2016, I reaped the best job I could ever have, because I wasn't doing anything wrong during that time. But now I look back on it, the mind is a terrible thing to waste especially when it's in the enemy's hands. You are left for dead. He had me thinking nobody loved me, that I couldn't trust anyone because they were talking about me. But really I was talking about myself because I didn't love me.

Chapter Six

Men & Robbery

This is the era of my ex-fiance Kaleb and I, when we were high on dope robbing places like Soup's Donuts with a be-be gun, up to the incident when I thought I was overdosing on cocaine and Xanax. We did get caught. But after getting from under those charges, I went on another robbery with him, where he hit a woman over the head with the fake gun. The guy who was in the store called 911 and told us not to move or go anywhere. But we ran to the car and left. The next day, someone called the cell. I'm thinking it's a girl calling for Kaleb. She asked for him and I told her "This is his wife." She said, "His wife??" I said, "Yes, his wife." At the time of this phone call, he and I were at his house, both high on Xanax. Then, there was knocking at the door and voices continuously shouting, "Police! Police! Open the door!" I was so scared when I heard them! I asked him, "Who is that?" He said that he didn't know but went to the door to see. I quickly began putting on my clothes while they were still banging and yelling for us to open the door. Kaleb was yelling back at them while getting himself together. The police said that they were there to get him. I couldn't understand other things they were saying because I was under the influence of a lot of handlebars (Xanax and muscle relaxers) mixed with alcohol.

Once inside, they had Kaleb in the front and ordered me to come out or they were going to send the dogs in. I don't remember exactly what my response was, but knowing me, I was probably talking a lot of mess to them. While I'm still getting dressed, the cop comes in the room. I said, "Excuse me!" I still had an attitude in the midst of getting arrested, tripping with a wicked mind. So I finished getting dressed and went to the front room but I wasn't handcuffed. Kaleb was. The police asked if they could take me downtown. I shook my head "Yes" because I'm still under the influence. As I'm answering the police, I saw Kaleb in the cop car telling me, "No! NO! Don't come down, stay there!" I was guessing that he needed me to get him out. But I wasn't thinking like that because I was under the influence and afraid, with so many cop cars being there and the big SWAT van in the driveway. Some people said that we were on the news that day. Well, I got in the cop car to leave, and standing outside I saw two super tall guys, taller than anyone else on the SWAT team. To this day, I believe they were my Guardian Angels because one of them said, "Is that her?" The other answered and said, "Yea, we finally got her."

Mind you, the police came for my ex, not for me. They were looking to see if I had anything to do with him. So, I'm riding in the car, unable to follow along and see where I am because I'm so high. We got to the facility and they told me I wasn't under arrest, but that they needed to ask me some questions. But I believed it was a trick because if I went in there and they started talking to me and I started to say the wrong things in response, then they would arrest me. Well, they took me to the interrogation room. When I snapped out of it, I saw two guys sitting on either side of the table with a recorder. The older guy had grey hair and his partner was bald. I could tell they were serious about their job. They started showing me pictures, asking me if that was me in them. I denied it every time they asked me. One of them said, "Well, you have on the same scrubs as the woman in the picture has." I hadn't even realized that when I had gotten dressed, I had put back on the same scrubs we did the robbery in. It's funny now, and I can laugh while I tell this story, but I knew that's when I needed saving. All that time, I was as high as the day was long. The last thing I remember clearly was that one of them asked me if that was me in the picture. I must have blacked out because the next thing I remembered, both of them were in my face, drilling me because they probably got the truth out of me at some point during the questioning. All I heard was talking in slow motion. Next thing I knew, I woke up in a holding cell, detox, with an orange and an egg in a bag. I panicked because I knew I was in jail. There was a phone in there on the wall and I tried to call Big Momma, but she wouldn't answer. When I finally reached her, I told her I was in jail. That's all I remember of the call. Shortly thereafter, I was moved back to general population with my attitude against everyone else of, "No, that's not me," among whole bunch of people like me; criminals, prostitutes, crackheads, all sleeping together in a little area. I started asking people what they were waiting on regarding the process. They told me about the list that let them know how much their bond will be. I found out my bond was $30,000, and everyone who had a bond over $5,000 had to be moved downtown. All the women sang songs during transport, making light of their situation, and I sang right alongside of them, looking crazy just like they were. When we got downtown, we had to appear in court, something I was not prepared for. The Judge told me I was arrested for twelve counts of robbery, and that my bond was $150,000. **Crickets**.... When I tell you that my eyes bucked so hard on the video stream...The people who were going to be seen after me got scared. They were asking me, "Man! What did you do?!?!" I went and sat down, leaving my bucked eyes where I stood. I couldn't see or hear anything. Everything was dead. After all was said and done, they took us through a tunnel to the elevator, and back to jail. The big, green iron door opened and there were women looking at me; different ages, different hair, but everyone was wearing orange. There were twelve women to each cell. When I got in the cell, I called my Big Momma and told her I needed a bail bondsmen. She said, "Baby don't you worry, Big Momma's gonna get you out." I said, "Yes ma'am." I'm on the phone and nervous because I didn't know why everyone was looking at me, probably because I was looking like I was scared. Once I finished talking to Big Momma, I went and climbed up on my top bunk and laid down. Looking around, I told myself, "This is not real. This isn't real." I had no control in this. And when I tell you that night when ten o'clock hit and those big heavy doors rolled shut by themselves, it was like, "Nette, you're in a completely different world, girlfriend."

Chapter Seven

Locked Up – My Way

So, there I was, locked up in County for eight months. Man, I saw a lot of stuff going on. The first two days I was there, I didn't really talk to anyone. On the third day, people approached me asking, "Hey, do you want this?" Or, "Give it to me if you're not gonna eat it." There was an older woman who said to me, "Baby, you're gonna have to eat something." I'm giving her this look as if to say, "You're somebody's Mother and you're in here, I'm not your baby." My attitude said to her and anyone else not to come over here by me and try to be my friend. I wasn't feeling that. But at the same time, I was scared. The woman kept looking at me then asked me, "Baby, what are you doing up in here?" My facial expression told her that I didn't have to tell her anything; then she eventually walked away.

After a couple of months passed, I lightened up on my attitude and began to talk to people to see what this place was about, and hung out with some of the women in the cell. I wanted to do things my way; I was hard-headed, flirtatious, purposefully talking to Caucasian women to have them buy me things from the Commissary. The situation finally got real to me after I was in that environment and seeing things I shouldn't have; women were mistreated during dorm shakedowns, and while they were held in the holding cell for court. Some women weren't fed or provided their hygiene needs while held there. And then we heard about someone who died on several occasions. It was like a whole new form of slavery in there, I felt, and I was exposed to that. I've witnessed women being shanked with razors; all of these things happened, but everyone in there was trying to go home. Some women did things their way, others did follow the rules. I was one who did it my way.

Big Momma wasn't coming through. I had been in there about two months as I constantly called and asked when I would get out. My court date came up, and I was escorted along with a group of women through the tunnel laughing the whole way, while everyone else was fearful. It still hadn't settled in my mind how real this situation really was. Court number "339" was the number for all of us who were charged with some form of robbery. We sat in the holding cell where those who had lawyers came and talked to their clients. My lawyer with glasses was a dork to me, because I felt like he wasn't trying to fight for me. Forgive me Lord. The space where the bailiff took us to talk to our lawyers wasn't private, so everyone in the holding cell could listen to all of our business. I couldn't stand that! You had NO privacy in jail. If anyone in there said that nobody knew their business, they were a liar. I could be in cell 55 and know what somebody did in cell 24. That's how it was. So my turn came to talk to my lawyer. "Hi Miss Pookie, I'm your court appointed attorney." That meant he was doing this job for free anyway. "Okay", I responded, not understanding what that meant back then. I found out later because of the knowledge God gave me while I was researching in there. He continued, "They have you for two counts of robbery, and that ranges from five to ninety nine years." I'm looking at him in disbelief…"Five? I can't do five years!" This man said, "The DA is offering you forty-five years." Forty-five years! Do you understand what I'm saying? I immediately broke down, and started telling all kind of lies; saying that I wasn't even helping him, he held a gun to my head, and he drugged me and made me go out there. I was so scared! We're talking about forty-five years here! I wasn't going to tell any truth, and no one was going to make me tell it either! They dropped the original twelve counts against me down to two counts of robbery by threat. I lied as hard and as much as I could to be believed. It was the fear in me. And in the Strength that took over me, I told my lawyer, "I'm not taking that deal!" I had never experienced Strength like that before. He said, "I'm going to do everything in my will to help you Ms. Pookie." "Yeah, right," was the attitude I had to his response.

After returning to the holding cell, I made up my mind I wasn't going to tell anyone about the forty-five years the DA offered; especially after hearing that some of the other women received only three years, two years, and even one year. One woman received eight months and she started to cry. I looked at her like, "Give me your eight months you don't want in exchange for this forty-five years!" Months passed and still tried to do it my way. Now, I have a girlfriend, so I don't have to worry about groceries. I started going to the education dorm, and then later to Church from there with others. I remember seeing this woman in the chapel, not knowing what she was talking about, but I didn't want to hear any of it. But then I started to listen to her, not realizing that's when God started talking to me while in jail even though I didn't pay attention. Then, my next court date came. The attorney came out and I thought I'd get some good news. He told me that they dropped the forty-five years down to fifteen years. OH NO! I'm not about to do fifteen years in here! I told him, "I'm not signing that paper!" So he went back and relayed my response to the DA. He returned and told me that he was able to get them to do a PSI, an investigation that included contacting my family members and employers. When it was time for me to return to court, they asked me all kind of questions about the robbery, but I lied on the stand. Afterwards, my Aunt took the stand, who I thought was going to be on my side, and she testified against me! "She was always a troublemaker and didn't listen." What did they call her on the stand for? She wanted me to be locked up so she wouldn't have to take care of me! When all the testimonies were done, the female judge said, "Pookie, I see you have been to different colleges. And it seems to me that you were capable of knowing that what you did was wrong." In my head I knew that wasn't going to go well at all. That woman told me she didn't care about me being a woman, and that I tried to use my gender to get out of it. The end result was two sevens concurrent. I didn't know what concurrent meant. So in my mind, she's giving me fourteen years. If I didn't sign the deal to take fifteen years, I surely wasn't going to sign for fourteen. But this case was different because of the PSI; so, regardless of the testimonies provided, the verdict was coming from the Judge, not a jury. And after finding out what *concurrent* meant, the total amount of time ordered was seven years. Lo, and behold, the lucky number seven, the number of completion. God gave me the number of completion. But at the time I didn't know it, and I still did things my way. I went back to my cell and cried my eyes out. Seven years! Aunt Laurie went home and told everybody that I got fourteen years. She didn't know what she was talking about, but I believed she thought, "Yeah, I got rid of her."

I'm back in the holding cell and my name gets called with others. It's time to get transported. I'm about to go to prison! Fear rose in me when I started to flash back on the mistreatment that I witnessed; and on top of that, the rumors about the Rose Unit there. I'm pleading from within that I don't get sent there. The enemy did a number on my mind, had me thinking that I would get killed in that unit. So, we got on the Bluebird, the white bus that was used for transport, still scared, and realized this was the first time I saw daylight in eight months. Everybody on the bus was smiling and laughing during the ride, but it was because they were finally outside. One of the worst experiences in my life was at Intake in the state jail. For some reason, they thought I was tried to sneak something in the facility inside my vaginal area. During the body search, they literally made me adjust and expose myself, and told me to cough. I got angry, held myself and asked in my shouting tone, "Do you see it? Is there something right there now??" Somewhat embarrassed, the guard then said that she didn't. After that horrible experience, they made us change out of our County clothes and put on an old-fashioned white gown with a number on it. Then off we went to the holding cell with our TDC badge that had our picture, name, birthdate, and our number. They escorted us to get examined, checked for physical disabilities and any gang affiliation, the latter being a very bad situation. This place was a different world from the County. No one is talked crazy or did anything at the moment. The environment seem more mature and more strict with their contraband search, and there was no unnecessary mistreatment. I got sent to another dorm, so scary. The dorms there didn't have a set time to get up, so we could sleep as long as we wanted. And that's exactly what I did during my first year there. I stayed to myself and I slept. So depressed. I missed my family, and was mad at them because nobody came to see me while I was locked up. It was like I was cast out. I eventually befriended a few women and began to get the layout of the prison, mainly the Commissary. It was much better there than in the County. Real food!

The Intake process prepares you for prison. That's where they hold you until it's time to send you to your unit, and there's a lot of transporting in and out through there. Of the five years I spent inside, I actually stayed in one place the last couple of years. They moved me around so much until that point, but I thank God for all that moving. I didn't get into trouble, but there were plenty of sheisty women in there and I didn't trust them. And I didn't stay to myself because I was trying to be fed, and I dated women to accomplish that. Lining up to eat was new to me. And there was a pill line for those who took meds at 4:00 am. Who is taking their pills at four in the morning?? I did start taking Seroquel after a while, illegally, after the dealers carried it their mouths to deliver it to me so I could put it in my cup. That's why I slept so much during my first year in, and one reason why I did things my way. I was in prison and on drugs; prison wasn't going to stop anything in there. But God had something in store for me. The Bluebird came for me and a few other women, and we were on our way from State Jail.

Chapter Eight

Locked Up 2 - Gods Plan

Now I'm in transit on the Bluebird to another unit and wind up at the first prison in Texas, where I grew up, right outside of my birth town. I felt so awkward being there. We were housed in the same place as the men but didn't see them because we were on the "A" side of the building, and they were on the "B" side on the transit floor. I didn't know I would be staying there forty two days because the staff didn't tell us that information. While there, I received a letter from the guy I was engaged to, who I played on with two women. He seemed hurt and upset that he was writing me while I was in prison, and after a while, he stopped writing me altogether. Still operating in my wicked mind, I made my cellmate climb up to the top bunk after she just had her baby. She almost whipped my tail when she found out that I was supposed to be on the top bunk and she had the bottom, so they ended up moving her.

Every other day, we would get called out for the Chaplain. So I would go, not really paying attention. God had a plan for me but I didn't care. I was still flirting with women, showing my behind, twerking...so much foolishness. The men at the unit were downstairs from us, and we would send kites (letters) to them; and in return, they would send us bubble gum and stuff. We would flush the toilets to talk to them, it was something about the pipe system, when the toilet flushed, we could hear each other through the pipes. I also adopted and performed the traditional calls of my Hispanic friends for attention, and they would pump me up so I would keep doing it, "Hey Pookie, do the 'gleeto'!" Just doing crazy stuff because we didn't have anything better to do. I also got my second tattoo (first prison tat) done in-house by one of my Hispanic friends.

On another day, we were called out again to go and listen to the Word of God. I really didn't care about it because I had just got done telling one woman what I was going to do to her; and I was still shooting kites to the men and also getting Commissary from them to occupy my day. The women kept trying to get me to go in with them. I told them that I was baptized at ten years old and I was good, using that as my excuse, and still being used by the enemy to get stuck in tradition that prevented me from having a real relationship with God. But on this day after giving in to go and listen, I was unaware of the special seed God was going to plant in me. This woman was speaking. And all I could think about was my hair being nappy, and when was somebody going to send me some money to get a perm. I really wasn't trying to hear what she was saying. Well, after she was done talking to us, everyone walked out and I was the last one to exit. But I got the urge to turn around and went over to look at a book. I figured that I didn't have anything else to read while being in the unit and I would be bored. So I took it. On the cover, there was a Bible on it. At first I thought it was a Jehovah Witness book. But I said to myself that I'll just read it anyway. Mind you, I'm not saved but I have something against Jehovah Witnesses because they're not right. Anybody else could tell me about the Word of God, but I wouldn't listen to them. There was something phony about them to me, not realizing that I was the phony one, not doing what I was supposed to do. I went back to my cell and began reading and came across the topic, "Questions about the Bible." In my mind I told myself that I already knew the Bible and that I was good; been baptized, grew up in Church...tradition. But as I continued reading, one verse caught my eye and changed my life in an instant. It read, "And God came down off His Throne and He was made into flesh, and He died on the Cross for us." Wait, didn't Jesus do that? A moment of confusion came across me. But out of nowhere, I received Knowledge of Wisdom. I pictured God as Jesus on the Cross and began to cry, telling God how sorry I was over and over again that He had to die on the Cross; just praying and crying nonstop. In that moment, I had acknowledged that the Father was the Son, and that the Son was the Father. To this day, I believe it was *that day* when I got saved.

A couple of weeks later, God showed me so many things while in that unit. He showed me a vision that let me know I was nowhere near where I needed to be. When I read that book, he showed me a vision with me in a place with a bright, golden colored light. But when I focused in on the light, there were faces in it, and they were smiling and looking at me. There were so many of them! It was like they had the Shekinah Glory on them that made them look like they were Gold; so many different, yet recognizable cultures all looking at me! While looking at that vision, I knew Jesus was God and God was Jesus, and I knew what I got with these visions was from God. He showed me these things in the cell. In the vision I could see me, and I had long, black hair. And I turned around and looked at me in the cell and winked my eye and smiled. I, too, was surrounded by the Shekinah Glory. And the clothing I wore was white as snow. God showed me that vision for a reason, and my life depended on finding out why He did. To this day, I know God added me to His Will right then. When I got out, I asked one of my Pastors why I felt like a got saved in the dorm instead of when I went to chapel 2weeks later and made it public. He told me it was because the Holy Spirit met you in that room. He said that when I acknowledged that the Father was the Son and the Son the Father, the Holy Spirit didn't have a choice but to meet me in that room because it was written.

Days after that life changing vision, I was transported to another holding, a place that appeared to be more sane in the environment. After being assigned to a dorm there, I began to have nightmares about Big Momma passing away. So when it came time to be called out for the Chaplain, I met this one woman in particular who came in that had the Shine on her, not like the other women that came and spoke to us. It was awesome! That was the first time I ever saw the Holy Spirit on someone! She was so beautiful, radiant, pure, and I knew she was a child of God. And I wanted that. I knew I wanted that! That day, April 9, 2009, when the woman asked if anyone wanted to rededicate their life, I went up to the altar. It was the first time I was hand in hand with the

Holy Spirit. I told her that she had a glow about her, and that I wanted what she had.

Prior to my rededication, I was in the dorm arguing with this woman who was heavily addicted to drugs, and that reminded me of my Mother. I took out all my anger on her, telling her that if my Mom was living that I wouldn't ever talk to her; and that I thought it was really sad that women abandoned their kids for drugs...really horrible things. This woman was a child of God who stayed to herself and in the Word. On a different night, I was going hard on her again about my Mom. This woman stopped what she was doing and told me, "There's not a day goes by that your Mom doesn't think about you." I shut up talking at that moment. I know now that God was speaking to me that day through her. I started to bombard her with a lot of "Why" questions about my Mom, and she would answer, "Ask God." Her responses prompted me to my first conversation with God that night. I asked Him, I cried, and I went to sleep. God was speaking through her to tell me to ask Him the questions I wanted to know the answers to. He told me, "Cry out to Me and ask Me anything you need to know." After that, when I saw that Glow on the woman, I knew I wanted God in my life as my Lord and Saviour because He saved me. He saved me from myself and He's still saving me today. I have a long track record with Him, but He is Faithful and Just and He'll do what He said because He loves me and I'm a part of the Beloved, His Ladybug. He always cared about me and never let me go. I know that's why He's having me write this book to remind me that He is my first Husband, my first Love.

I wasn't the same after I rededicated my life to God that day. Every day I would get up and pray and read my Bible, and I would read until I fell asleep. Everytime I read something, I would speak on it. But I was still struggling with homosexuality. Until one day, God woke me up and asked, "Why do you go with women?" He was so blunt in his asking! He said that they have the same things I have. I told Him that He was right and that was nasty. So, that day God delivered me from homosexuality. Oh how I loved to spend time with Him through His Word and praying! I didn't have anything to worry about because His Word says that He protects me while I sleep, and His Angels watch over me and I knew I had a purpose, a greater purpose, made to do greatness and be great but only through the Word and Spirit of God. It was all His idea, and His ideas are awesome! They always come through.

During that time in prison, I grew in God. I fasted and prayed, learned how to be patient, and made new Godly friends. I attended Vine Bible College in prison, still experiencing ups and downs, but I learned that God is not a chain of command by the book titled *The Shack*. I read about the Holy Spirit from Benny Hinn's books, about fasting and speaking in the Spirit. I just love God! I talked to people about Jesus. I felt everyone needed to be a part of this! They needed to know that God loved them and that He (Abba) and the Holy Spirit were real; that He would saved them and they would have peaceful rest. They could have joy being used by God, and that meant His Kingdom would grow. He doesn't lie. He gives restoration, words to pray, and zeal for His Word and discernment. He always watches out for you. I remember one time in prison when I was on the "hoe squad" working in the field. I didn't have clothes to go out that Monday, and I would get in trouble because of that. That weekend I pulled on God, "You said that if I call on you and ask you for anything, then you would give it. I don't know how you're gonna get these clothes but please get me these clothes." Five minutes later, the woman in charge of the clothes came back after five hours from being off shift and gave me what I needed. People I told this to tried to downplay it like it wasn't a big thing. But in prison, that's huge. There was so much Merciful Favor in prison with the jobs I had. God is still in the miracle and favor business. At the end of my trial in prison I learned and lived, and I knew He was Faithful. My parole was denied countless times, but God did it for me in the end and I was released to go home. I thank God for everything I learned while in prison.

Chapter Nine

Under A New Rule & New Trust

The reason I call this chapter Under A New Rule is because now I'm back in the world after being in prison, and I'm saved this time. I'm under a completely different Reign, Ruled by God. Different life. Different perspective. Different idea. I'm seeing things through God's eyes and not my own, not looking at life the way I was when I was lost and not realizing how valuable life really was; and that I was made for greater. God wants me to talk about how I acted under His New Rule: the Kingdom of God and of Jesus Christ, my Lord and Savior, a Trusting God. I trusted God in prison, and sometimes I was tested. But when I got out, I was tested even more. So I had to really, really, REALLY trust in God. He showed me that I was under Supernaturally Divine Training, in other words, He was training me in His Word.

After I got saved and began reading His Word, God began showing me different things, like how to handle situations through Him and His Word only. What I mean by that is when I was in prison, I used to wake up every morning and read His Word. Although the guards woke us up at 4:00 am, I was already awake before then at 3:00 am. God would wake me up at 3:00 in the morning and put me on my knees to pray. He was showing me how to get up and read His Word, and talked to me through it. I was in love with the Word of God after I got saved. And if someone misquoted the scripture, I would be the first to tell them, "That's not what the Word says;" my favorite saying. I was on fire for God, so much zeal was in me for Him. The Holy Spirit had given me revelation and understanding of His Word, that was something I learned as I began reading. I spent time in His Word, even though I was in prison and could have been doing other things. God was building my foundation.

Becoming familiar with the Holy Spirit, knowing that the Holy Spirit was my helper, I could pray in the Spirit when I didn't know what to pray for. When I first got saved, I had a passion to learn to pray in the spirit. While in prison, I was baptized with the Holy Spirit. One day, a few of the women and I were in a circle talking, and I told them that I wanted to speak in the spirit. It was such a hunger within me to be able to do this, not even knowing that doing so would take me to a deeper level with God. The Word of God says that I can pray and no one else will know what I'm praying except for the Holy Spirit and God. That was so intriguing to me, yet so trustworthy of God. It was a solid rock for me to stand on so I wouldn't fall, and I was giving complete access and control to the Holy Spirit to rule in my life. That's why I wanted so badly to speak in the spirit. What I knew was that I didn't know what to pray for, but the Holy Spirit did and I could trust Him and learn so much more about Him. I wanted to please God. I had to please Him because He saved me. There's the old saying, "I love God because He first loved me." That's TRUE! That's why we love God, and there's nothing to be ashamed of. It is what the Word of God says, the Logos, the Breath of God, the Rema. It is the Living Word in effect right now in the life of phenomenal, radical, apostolic Christians. That is what makes us Move, wanting to please God because He loved us.

The Holy Spirit began to discipline me through speaking in the spirit of God, the utterance. Through the Holy Spirit, I started to have a passion for fasting. Fasting and speaking in the spirit is like a double dose of Power; it's that Holy Spirit, Kingdom shaking, 'Satan you don't have nothing to stand on' kind of power. So God began to teach me about fasting; the three and seven day fasts. I did two seven-day fasts in prison, and did a lot of three-day fasts. Pastor Jenice would always say, "If you're having a problem, put 'three' on it." That's real. I was doing the three-day fasts before I started going to the Church in prison. My routine was that I would fast, feel good, and get into the Word. And there were more powerful revelations after that. Then I started having dreams. The Lord gave me dreams and visited me in them. He even had Angels come and visit me in my dreams. I would hear God talk over and whisper within me. I even heard the Holy Spirit pray for me in my sleep! It was so awesome! Next, I began to work in His miracles. God would heal people through me. There was a woman who was limping, and I began to pray for her while God touched her back. After the prayer, the woman was shocked and surprised, saying that her back felt better and good. And everyone who was around was amazed. This woman started going to Church after that. Everyone I came in contact with who really didn't go to Church would get a taste of the Gospel from me. I started to spread what God gave me. He would always put the Word in my spirit and taught me how to talk to people in their different situations that I never knew. But every time I spoke, I knew that the Holy Spirit was speaking through me. All of this was a result of me rejoicing in the things that were talked about in God's Word. I was so radical for God, and I know He's restoring that zeal and radicalness within me in Jesus Name.

God was renewing my mind. He gave me education by downloading three years of high school that I didn't pass because of my reading, grammar and communication, and He helped me with it all. I took the THEA test and missed the passing Math score by four points. But I passed the reading and was eligible to start my college classes. I took two vocational classes and passed them both. God did so much, He restored my soul. It was a process God took me through on HIS time. He was mending and humbling me in prison. So when I got out, I made a vow to do right by God. I was now under a New Rule. I was so grateful for EVERYTHING; grateful for being out and making $9 and something at Wendy's, and able to be in the House of the Lord shouting, lifting up and Praising God. I was on fire for that!

Then the tests and trials began to come. Everything that God delivered me from was trying to come back. Some of those tests I failed, but some I passed. I passed with drugs although I tried to smoke, now after being saved and knowing what I was doing. But I couldn't smoke it right. I was always convicted, so I had to stop. I started back drinking, which was a big issue for me, and just recently stopped a couple of months ago. I don't want it anymore. I don't want any of it. God had to sit me down, and allow doors to open to create a thorn in my flesh. Men were my weakness and my flesh caused me to marry the wrong man. I'm going through a divorce right now because I was hard-headed. God told me this wasn't the man He had for me, but I fell in love anyway and got hurt. But God is Faithful and Just, and as I record this book I'm still learning. That's how awesome He is! I'm telling y'all all of this because the same processes and things I dealt with in prison are the same for me now, and I love it! Sometimes I do get annoyed. For example, I was listening to the original audio version of this book, and there was a part that said I needed to forgive myself, the one person I still need to forgive in the Name of Jesus, but God is still working on me. HE IS AN AWESOME GOD! I'm not where I need to be right now, but THANK GOD I'm not where I used to be. I was down, lost, and under a different rule. But now I'm under a New Rule; Kingdom, that is the Kingdom of God, the Kingdom of Victory in the Name of Jesus. Thank You Lord! After going through all these processes, God brought me to a complete standstill; still having all His Grace and Mercy, but not all His Blessings simply because of disobedience and backsliding. When I got out of prison, I went back to some of my old habits, but in 2015, my Blessed life was refreshed under a New Rule.

Chapter Ten

Forgiveness/In Gods Charge

In the last chapter I talked about how God used me, by filling me with the zeal and passion to help do wonders in His Kingdom. This chapter will also show you that we do fall. This is not a chapter of excuses. It's a chapter that will get you to understand why Jesus came down and died on the cross for us anyway. We can't do this life by ourselves, because when we try, we fall. This chapter is about forgiveness and being in God's charge. The reason I'm talking about forgiveness is because I'm revealing that I still had unforgiveness in my heart towards some people. Yes, I was saved, but I didn't realize there was still residue of that after my fall. I was unforgiving toward my family all over again after being out of prison. When times got tough, I was leaning on my own knowledge that was wicked, instead of seeking God like I had been doing. I was out and free, but the real life tests started to come forth while being under this New Rule, even with my fire for God.

In the last chapter, I talked about my fall in drinking and smoking. In 2015, I was in a marriage that was not ordained by God, and with a man who wasn't a man of God. And I tried so hard to make him a man of God. But this isn't about my ruined marriage or what people did to me. It's about what I did and didn't do. What I didn't do was seek God during my trial-and-error period of my walk in God. I began to rely on my own knowledge, figuring since I knew the Word of God I had it under control. And what happened when I was in that frame of mind was I started to believe I didn't need the Word of God anymore. I could pick it up and spend time with Him when I felt like it. This is real talk right here. I was free, working, still loving God, but I'm getting angry because people aren't doing and being what and who I think they should do and be. This is all wicked wisdom, fleshly thinking. It has nothing to do with seeking God. This is a time in my life of failure and where I forgot to trust God. He got me. He knew me and knew what I was going through. But instead of seeking Him the way I was in prison and with fasting, I was too busy trying to enjoy the freedom under this New Rule; all the while I was straddling the fence...being saved but wanted to live worldly. I knew how to live my life. It was as if to say, "Thank you God, you brought me this far. I'm under a New Rule and I know how to do it now. I don't need your help." But that was a lie from the enemy, and my state of mind in 2015 under wicked wisdom, meaning that I relied on my own wisdom and not the everlasting Word of God. But I knew God and was filled with the Holy Spirit, saved. The devil is a LIE if people say that the ones who are saved and filled with the Holy Spirit don't fall. That's a lie from the pits of hell.

During the trial-and-error periods of life, God is teaching you how to rely on and trust in Him. He teaches you to allow Him to take charge of your life. When I was in prison, I was under the process of His instructions. Now, I'm out but on the battlefield of my mind. And I started to walk on that battlefield with wicked wisdom making me forget the Word of God and fall. I thought I knew everything, but I didn't. God had to bring me back to Him. In April of 2015, a woman named Jamie, known to many as Momma Dee, called my Aunt to see if she wanted to come and visit Free Indeed. We were introduced to Free Indeed by my Aunt's ex-husband Bobby, who met the Apostle the Church's Prison Ministry. So, I got an invitation to go with them. At that time, I had fallen back to drinking, and was wondering why God left me because I was struggling with my husband who didn't want to work. He contributed a little bit, but I was the one who really struggled and believed in God to get us through this thing, and He did. (Anyway back to the book) Well, I got picked up and we went to a weekend retreat in, Texas, that the church was hosting. It was so awesome! Freedom Weekend was the name of the retreat and the Lord began to minister to me before I even got to the Church. I didn't know what was going on, and didn't know anybody. On the way to the retreat, I sat next to Katy and Pam, two mighty women of God. We arrived, and we praise God together the whole weekend. I loved every song I heard, and my response from within was like, "Oh my God! This is what I needed!" Each day was a different day, but during those days, God broke chains off of me. During my battle with wicked wisdom, I didn't realize that I wasn't fully forgiving in my spirit, because I still had unforgiveness toward my Aunt Laurie who had testified against me during my trial, and her Step-brother who attempted to molest me. God revealed all that to me at the retreat. I finally forgave her. And when I did, she later came and told me that she didn't know about her brother's attempts on me. For her to come to me and apologize about this, that broke a lot of chains and opened a lot of doors. Ever since then, I was back and forth from Free Indeed, still going through it with my marriage, but I kept holding on to my Church and God, He wanted me to keep holding on to it and Him. God began to minister awesome things to me through Free Indeed and that Ministry. And He also began to minister directly to me. He got me back to fasting and being in His Word. He brought me back, and now God's in charge.

I know this book may not be what people consider as drastic, but it is meant for ordinary people who are made extraordinary through the Blood of Jesus Christ, and walk in the Supernatural and hear the voice of God. God brought me back and strongholds were destroyed at the retreat. Three months ago I rededicated my life, and God said that He honored that. This book doesn't have an ending, Thank You Jesus, because my life has not ended. That's what I meant by God is still working on me. He delivered me from wicked wisdom and the chokehold of the enemy. Another thing God has done is He helped me to forgive myself. He has taught me how to not listen to the lies of the enemy, and that I'm made for great things. That's what His Word says. "The Lord is my Shepherd I shall not want. He maketh me lie down in green pastures. He leadeth me beside the still waters. He restoreth my soul. He leadeth me in the path of Righteousness for His Namesake. Yea, though I walk in the valley of the shadow of death, I will fear no evil, for Thou art with me, Thy rod and Thy staff they comfort me.Thou preparest a table before me in the presence of mine enemies,

Thou anointest my head with oil, my cup runneth over. Surely goodness and mercy shall follow me all the days of my life, and I will dwell in the house of the Lord Forever. Amen" (Psalms 23).

I will dwell in the house of the Lord forever because He continues to work on me and build me up. And He will do the same thing for you. He's a Counselor; Provider, He provides for His kids and won't let them go without. And if something is taken away, that's because He has something better for you. God's In Charge! Allow God to be in charge of your life! When you receive Jesus Christ as your Lord and Savior, you're saying, "God, I trust you." Lord means "Ruler" and "Master". You are under God's Charge. WE are under God's charge. We have to stay underneath the Charge. That keeps us in the Will of the Greater Kingdom, with the Greater Kingdom being the Word of God; the Logos, and He moves on the Rhema Word through His ministering Angels. We have to stay under that Rule, the Rule of the Greater Kingdom; the Kingdom of Jesus Christ; of Abba, the Father; of the Holy Spirit; of the Ministering Angels who protect us. Every day, I want you to do this: to put on the whole armor of God. Ephesians 6:13-20 says, "Therefore, take up the whole armor of God, that you may be able to withstand in the evil day, having done all, to stand. Stand therefore having girded your waist with truth, having put on the breastplate of righteousness and having shod your feet with the preparation of the Gospel of Peace, Jesus Christ. Above all, taking the shield of Faith with which you will be able to quench all the fiery darts of the wicked one, and take the helmet of salvation and the sword of the spirit which is the Word of God. Praying always in all prayer and supplication in the spirit being watchful to this end with all perseverance and supplication of all the saints. And for me, that utterance may be given to me that I may open my mouth boldly to make known the mystery of the Gospel for which I am an ambassador in chains, and that I may speak as boldly as I ought to."

Now, let's break down the armor of God: the Helmet of Salvation represents that you know you are a child of God, you belong to Jesus Christ because you gave your life to Him to allow Him to be Lord and Master over you. In your mind are things of God and not things of this wicked world. The Breastplate of Righteousness represents that you know that you're not standing before God with any sin, but that you're sin-free through repentance, and believe in your heart. He guards your heart with the breastplate of righteousness because you are justified by Christ's blood. The Belt of Truth covers your loins, and to me, that represents where deep secrets of life are kept, which Christ purged from you. After purging, He plants new things within you so they can blossom and be what they need to be in your life. You are guarded by the belt of truth, that holds the Sword which is the Word of God. Your truth is revealed by the Word of God; you walk in that truth because you know the Word and what it says about you. When I think about preparing my feet with the Gospel of Jesus Christ, that means being ready to tell anybody about Him, about what He has done for me; giving people my testimony, letting them know that He continues to work on my mind and in my heart, so that I won't lose sight of His Will for my greatness. The Shield of Faith protects you from the fiery darts every hour of the day. It represents believing every Word He has shown to you, and spoken to you, and whispered to you in your sleep. You walk in it and the enemy can't tear you down because that shield of Faith is protecting you. The last piece of armor is the Sword that is the Word of God. We need that. It connects us to the Vine. It purges us and increases our walk with God, and opens our eyes and ears to know His voice. His Word says, "My sheep know My Voice…." We are under God's Charge.

I came from being born in a welfare hospital to a woman who was locked up; living with a Grandmother who could barely hold me and keep me because of her aging; living with an Aunt who allowed her brother to molest me and who testified against me; being with guys who I thought loved me but really didn't; committing crimes of robbery with these men; homosexuality over an eight year span, and was engaged for a short time during that span; a background of evil thinking including suicide, not allowing people into my life for fear of rejection; being hateful, arrogant, selfish; being ruled by my mind that was being ruled by the enemy of darkness, a hierarchy; doing witchcraft to become pregnant, masturbation, and using sex as my hero. These are all the things that God has delivered me from. And I will tell you this: if He can deliver me, He can deliver you. He is Faithful and Just to do it. No matter what it looks like, He will do it. I wasn't in a good place when

I went to God. I was still dealing with homosexuality, and was evil. But God touched me. He changed me. I wasn't changed when I went to God. I wasn't even ready. But I took that step because I didn't want to live the way I was living. I wasn't good. I didn't just go to Church one day and say I was ready to live for God; I didn't do that. That's not accurate because everybody doesn't do that. God released me from the fire, and if He can release me He can release you. He has already paid the price for our sins. People, we have got to stop using excuses to try and get ourselves together! Let's do a one-on-one with the Holy Spirit. Allow Him to come into your life and change you. Change isn't bad, it's for YOU, not for God. Salvation is for YOU, not for God. He loves you, and He has a plan for you. If He didn't, the enemy wouldn't be taking you through so much. And for some of you, the enemy thinks he has you but he doesn't. Jesus Loves You, from the moment you wake up until you lay down, no matter where you are in life. Come to Him and let Him cleanse you. It doesn't matter if you're in a same-sex marriage/relationship, smoking or getting high, drinking, having an affair, upset by an argument with your mom, or if you just stole something or tried to commit suicide, and you're reading this book; this book is for you. God is talking to you. He wants you to be with Him. He Loves You. Come back.

Prayer of Salvation

This is a prayer for those who want to do something different, whether you are living the way I did or not. Jesus is for Everybody. I just want you to repeat after me and know that this is something that you want, for Jesus to come into your heart as your Lord and Savior to lead and guide you, and prepare you for your great destiny He called forth for you in His Will. Read this out loud and the Holy Spirit will hear and answer you; the Father, Son, and the Holy Spirit. He Loves you and wants better for you; not for you to be mediocre in this life. He wants you to be great in Him. If it's just being great in love, humility, healing, teaching, evangelizing, prophecy, apostleship, as a listener and praying for people, or fasting, let Him Love you; bless you; build you up and take your burdens away. He said that His yoke is easy and His burdens are light. Let Him be your Peace among destruction. And most importantly, allow Him to save you from yourself like He did for me.

Repeat after me: Lord Jesus, I confess with my mouth and believe in my heart that you are God, and you came down into flesh and died on the cross for my sins. And after you died, you rose again on the third day. This I do believe. Lord God, I ask you to come into my life as my Lord and Savior, Master and Ruler, to forgive me of my sins, known and unknown. Thank you Jesus for coming into my life to forgive me for and saving me from my sins. In Jesus Name, Amen.

Once you pray this prayer, God will come into your heart and begin to move and shape you. It may be a quick impact, or it may be a slow encounter like it was for me. But know that He's there now, and you are a part of a Greater Kingdom. We have already won. We're just waiting for the bell to ring. God Bless you.

Love you,
Pookie

Printed in the United States
By Bookmasters